19 KEYS TO FAST SALES

CLOSING DEALS QUICKLY

By

DOUGLAS GARY

Table Of Contents

Chapter 4

Introduction

The Importance Of Closing Deals Quickly

Closing deals quickly is a critical factor in the success of any business, with several benefits contributing to its growth and sustainability. We will now take a closer look at these advantages.

Firstly, closing deals quickly enables businesses to generate revenue faster, which is crucial in today's fast-paced business environment. A delay in closing deals increases the likelihood of customers changing their minds or finding competitors. Therefore, swift deal closure is necessary to secure the revenue needed for growth and expansion.

Secondly, closing deals quickly provides businesses with a competitive advantage by demonstrating their commitment to responsiveness and efficiency. In a competitive market where customers have numerous options, reliability and efficiency go a long way in attracting repeat business.

Thirdly, swift deal closure results in improved cash flow as businesses can receive payment faster. This improvement in cash flow allows businesses to reinvest, pay down debts or capitalise on new opportunities, leading to sustainable growth and profitability.

Fourthly, lengthy deal closures result in increased costs associated with maintaining them. Sales and marketing efforts may need to be extended, contracts renegotiated, or administrative costs increased, which can add up over time. By closing deals quickly, businesses can save on costs, freeing up resources to focus on other areas of their operations.

Lastly, swift deal closure is beneficial for customers, leading to enhanced customer satisfaction. Customers appreciate prompt service and the speedy resolution of their needs. By demonstrating a commitment to customer satisfaction, businesses can build positive relationships, leading to repeat business and referrals.

In conclusion, closing deals quickly is essential for the growth and success of any business. It increases revenue, provides a competitive advantage, improves cash flow, reduces costs, and enhances customer satisfaction. Businesses that prioritise swift deal closure position themselves for long-term success and sustainability.

Chapter 1

Key #1: Build Rapport With The Customer

Establishing a connection with customers is the cornerstone of building rapport. It involves fostering a sense of trust and understanding, which can make customers feel more comfortable and receptive to your offerings. By building rapport, you're not just selling a product or service, but rather creating a relationship that can result in repeat business and referrals.

Active listening is a crucial component of building rapport. It entails paying close attention to both verbal and nonverbal cues from the customer. Demonstrating an interest in their needs and concerns can create a sense of trust and empathy.

Finding common ground with the customer is another important aspect of building rapport. This may involve shared interests or experiences, allowing for the establishment of a deeper connection.

Positive body language also plays a vital role in building rapport. A warm smile, consistent eye contact, and open body language can foster a sense of approachability and friendliness, making the customer more open to your message.

Empathy is key to building rapport, involving putting yourself in the customer's shoes and understanding their perspective. By recognizing their feelings and concerns, you can establish a sense of trust and understanding.

Lastly, being authentic is essential to building rapport. Customers can often detect insincerity or inauthenticity, so it's important to show genuine interest in their needs and desires to establish trust and create a solid foundation for a long-term relationship.

In conclusion, building rapport with customers relies on creating a connection based on trust, understanding, and empathy. Through active listening, finding common ground, using positive body language, demonstrating empathy, and being authentic, you can establish a strong rapport with customers and improve your chances of closing deals efficiently.

Key #2: Ask The Right Questions

Another crucial factor in closing deals quickly is the ability to ask the right questions. By asking the right questions, you can collect valuable information about your customer's needs and concerns, which can help you customise your sales pitch and address any objections they may have. Below are a few suggestions on how to ask appropriate questions:

Begin with open-ended questions: Ask questions that cannot be answered with a simple "yes" or "no." These questions encourage the customer to provide more details, which can help you comprehend their needs and desires better. Example. "Could you please provide me more details of what you seek."?

Use probing questions: Follow-up questions that assist you in obtaining more information about a specific topic are known as probing questions. For instance, if a customer expresses interest in a particular product, you could ask, "What about that product appeals to you?"

Inquire about pain points: Pain points refer to the issues or difficulties that the customer is facing. By asking about their pain points, you can gain a better understanding of their needs and concerns. As an example, a question you could ask is, "What difficulties or obstacles are you encountering with your present solution?"

Be specific: Don't be afraid to ask detailed questions about the customer's needs and wants. The more specific you are, the better you can tailor your sales pitch to meet their needs. One way to approach this would be to pose questions like, "What is the frequency of product usage you anticipate?"

Avoid leading questions: Leading questions imply a particular answer and can be off-putting to customers. They can also make it appear that you are not genuinely interested in their needs. Instead, ask neutral questions that allow the customer to provide honest and open answers.

Asking the right questions requires practice, but it can be a powerful tool for closing deals quickly. By starting with open-ended questions, using probing questions, asking about pain points, being specific, and avoiding leading questions, you can gather critical information about the customer's needs and concerns and customise your sales pitch accordingly.

Key #3: Listen Carefully To The Customer's Needs

Paying close attention to the customer's needs is a crucial element of successful sales. When you actively listen to the customer, you gain a better understanding of their challenges, objectives, and motivations, enabling you to customise your sales presentation and offer a solution that meets their specific requirements. Here are some additional suggestions for expanding on the key points discussed above:

Offer the customer your complete attention: This means being present and avoiding any distractions. Turn off your phone and shut down any other applications that may divert your attention. Being fully engaged demonstrates to the customer that you value their time and input.

Avoid interrupting: Interrupting the customer can be impolite and may impede your ability to fully comprehend their needs. It's critical to let the customer finish their thoughts before responding. This also demonstrates active listening and provides them with the opportunity to express their ideas fully.

Ask for clarification: If you don't fully comprehend something the customer is saying, don't hesitate to ask for clarification. This indicates that you are actively involved in the conversation and interested in understanding their viewpoint. You may ask open-ended questions such as "Can you tell me more about that?" or "How does that impact your business?"

Paraphrase and summarise: To ensure that you understand the customer's needs, you may summarise or paraphrase what they've stated. This ensures that you're both on the same page and helps you tailor your sales pitch to their specific concerns. For instance, "So, if I understand correctly, you're seeking a solution that can boost your team's productivity while also reducing costs."

Observe nonverbal cues: Pay attention to the customer's body language, tone of voice, and facial expressions. These can provide additional insights into their needs and emotions. For example, if the customer appears hesitant or unsure, you may want to ask more questions to clarify their concerns.

Display empathy: Empathy is the ability to understand and share the emotions of others. By demonstrating empathy, you show that you care about the customer and are committed to assisting them in finding a solution that meets their needs. You may demonstrate empathy by acknowledging the customer's concerns and expressing a genuine interest in their success.

To conclude, listening carefully to the customer's needs is a vital skill for closing deals quickly. By offering the customer your complete attention, avoiding interruptions, asking for clarification, paraphrasing and summarising, observing nonverbal cues, and showing empathy, you can gain a better understanding of their needs and tailor your sales pitch to address their specific concerns.

Key #4: Demonstrate Your Product Or Service

When demonstrating your product or service, it's crucial to remember that the primary objective is to exhibit how it can provide value to the customer. Below are some additional tips to expand on the aforementioned points:

Personalise the demo to the customer: Before the demo, conduct research on the customer's business and understand their distinct challenges and priorities. This will enable you to customise the demo to their specific needs and demonstrate how your product or service can resolve their specific issues.

Emphasise benefits over features: Although highlighting the features of your product or service is important, explaining how those features can benefit the customer is equally critical. For instance, if you're selling software, don't only talk about the features, such as the number of functions or tools it has. Instead, emphasise the benefits, such as how it can save the customer time, enhance productivity, or reduce costs.

Keep it straightforward: While you may be tempted to showcase every feature or function of your product or service during the demo, it's essential to keep it simple and concentrate on the most important aspects. Stick to the key benefits and features that will be most relevant to the customer's needs.

Anticipate objections: Consider any concerns or objections the customer may have and proactively address them during the demo. This can help to establish trust and confidence in your product or service. For example, if the customer is concerned about the cost, be prepared to explain how the benefits of your product or service can outweigh the cost.

Encourage engagement: Inviting the customer to interact with the product or service during the demo can help to increase their engagement and interest. Allow them to try out the product or service for themselves and ask questions along the way. This can help to build their confidence in the product or service.

Follow up: After the demo, follow up with the customer to address any remaining questions they may have and to continue the conversation about how your product or service can assist them. This can help to maintain the momentum and increase the chances of closing the deal quickly.

In conclusion, demonstrating your product or service can be an effective way to show the customer how it can provide value to them. By personalising the demo to the customer, emphasising benefits, keeping it straightforward, anticipating objections, encouraging engagement, and following up, you can enhance your chances of closing the deal quickly.

Key #5: Highlight Your Unique Selling Points

To close deals quickly, it's essential to highlight your unique selling points (USPs). These are the features or benefits of your product or service that differentiate it from your competitors and make it the optimal choice for the customer. Follow these guidelines to effectively showcase your USPs:

Investigate your competition: Before highlighting your USPs, research your competition to gain an understanding of what they offer and how they position themselves. This will help you identify your own unique strengths and weaknesses.

Comprehend your customer's needs: To effectively highlight your USPs, you must comprehend your customer's needs and priorities. This will allow you to tailor your message to their specific concerns and demonstrate how your product or service can address their problems.

Emphasise the benefits: When highlighting your USPs, focus on the benefits they provide, rather than just the features. For instance, if your USP is that your product is eco-friendly, explain how this benefits the customer and the environment, rather than just stating that it's a feature of the product.

Use stories and examples: Stories and examples can help bring your USPs to life and make them more memorable for the customer. For instance, if your USP is that your service is more dependable than your competitors, recount a story about how your service saved a customer from a costly outage.

Use visual aids: Visual aids, such as charts, graphs, or infographics, can help illustrate your USPs and make them more compelling for the customer.

Be confident: When highlighting your USPs, be confident and enthusiastic. Show the customer that you truly believe in your product or service and that it's the best choice for them.

In conclusion, effectively communicating your USPs is critical to swiftly closing deals. By investigating your competition, comprehending your customer's needs, emphasising the benefits, using stories and examples, using visual aids, and being confident

Chapter 2

Key #6: Address Objections Head-On

Effectively handling objections is an essential step towards quickly closing deals. Objections are concerns or doubts that potential customers may have regarding your product or service, and if left unaddressed, they can result in missed sales opportunities. To effectively address objections, the following tips can be helpful:

Anticipate objections: Prior to meeting with the customer, try to anticipate any objections that they might have based on their past experiences, concerns, or needs. This will allow you to prepare a response that addresses their objections before they even raise them.

Listen actively: When a customer raises an objection, listen carefully to what they are saying and demonstrate that you understand their concerns. This can help build trust and rapport with the customer.

Respond confidently: When responding to objections, be assertive and confident. Show the customer that you understand their concerns and have a solution that caters to their specific needs.

Use proof points: To back up your claims and demonstrate that your product or service can overcome their objections, use statistics, customer testimonials, or case studies.

Reframe objections as questions: Some objections can be reframed as questions that you can answer with your unique selling points. For example, if a customer expresses doubts about your product's reliability, you could highlight your product's reliability as one of its unique selling points.

Avoid defensiveness: It's crucial not to become defensive when addressing objections. Instead, approach objections as an opportunity to understand the customer's needs better and concerns, and provide them with the information they need to make an informed decision.

In conclusion, effectively addressing objections head-on is an integral part of closing deals quickly. By anticipating objections, actively listening to customers, responding confidently, using proof points, reframing objections as questions, and avoiding defensiveness, you can effectively overcome objections and convince customers to choose your product or service.

Key #7: Create A Sense Of Urgency

Generating a sense of urgency is a potent sales strategy that can hasten deal closures. It encourages customers to make purchase decisions promptly and avoid procrastination. Below are some methods to create a sense of urgency:

Time-limited offers: Proposing a discount or promotion with a limited duration can stimulate a sense of urgency and prompt the customer to make a swift purchase decision.

Limited stock availability: If a particular product or service has a restricted inventory, informing the customer can stimulate a sense of urgency and encourage them to make a prompt purchase before it runs out.

FOMO: Fear of missing out is a persuasive motivator. By highlighting the advantages of your product or service and emphasising the potential drawbacks of not taking advantage of the opportunity, you can create a sense of urgency.

Deadline reminders: If the purchase has a deadline, such as a product launch or a time-limited promotion, reminding the customer can stimulate a sense of urgency and encourage them to make a prompt purchase decision before it is too late.

Limited availability of your time: If you are a service provider, highlighting your busy schedule and limited availability can generate a sense of urgency and encourage the customer to book your services quickly.

Highlighting the consequences of delay: Delays in making a purchase can result in negative consequences such as missing out on a limited-time promotion or increased prices. By emphasising these consequences, you can stimulate a sense of urgency and encourage the customer to make a prompt purchase decision.

In conclusion, creating a sense of urgency is a potent sales technique that can accelerate deal closures. By using limited-time promotions, highlighting limited stock availability, inducing FOMO, setting deadline reminders, emphasising your limited availability, and highlighting the consequences of delay, you can encourage customers to make purchase decisions promptly.

Key #8: Offer Incentives Or Discounts

Providing incentives or discounts is a proven approach to motivating customers to make a purchase decision. The idea is to offer additional value to customers, which can encourage them to take action and make a purchase. Below are further details about each type of incentive or discount:

Percentage discounts: This type of incentive is popular, where a percentage is discounted from the regular price of a product or service. This discount can either be a flat percentage off the price or can vary based on the purchase value or quantity. For example, you may offer a 10% discount on all purchases for a limited time or a 20% discount on orders over a specific amount.

Buy-one-get-one-free offers: This incentive is commonly used to motivate customers to purchase more than one product. It can be effective for products that are frequently bought in multiples, such as food or beauty products. For instance, a customer may buy a shampoo and receive a conditioner for free.

Bundle offers: This incentive involves bundling several products or services into a single package and providing a discount on the overall price. It can be a compelling way to motivate customers to buy more products or services from your business. For example, you might offer a discount when a customer purchases a bundle of services, such as web design and hosting services.

Referral discounts: This incentive rewards customers for referring others to your business. Both the customer who makes the referral and the new customer who is referred can receive referral discounts. This can be an effective way to enhance customer loyalty and attract new customers to your business.

Loyalty rewards: This incentive is designed to reward customers for their loyalty and repeat purchases. It can include discounts or free products for customers who make a specific number of purchases, or special perks for long-term customers. Loyalty rewards can help build customer loyalty and encourage customers to continue doing business with your company.

Early bird discounts: This incentive offers customers a discount if they make a purchase early. It can be effective for promoting new products or services or incentivizing customers to buy during a pre-sale period. Early bird discounts can help increase sales and generate buzz for your business.

Overall, offering incentives or discounts can be an effective approach to motivate customers to make a purchase decision. When used strategically, these incentives and discounts can help close deals quickly and increase customer loyalty.

Key #9: Provide Social Proof

Using social proof is an effective sales technique that can help you establish trust and credibility with potential customers, thereby closing deals quickly. Social proof is based on the idea that people are more likely to follow the actions of others, especially those whom they perceive as similar to themselves or whom they trust. Here are some methods to incorporate social proof into your sales strategy:

Customer testimonials: Collecting feedback from satisfied customers and sharing their testimonials is an effective way to promote your product or service. These testimonials can be displayed on your website, social media pages, or in marketing materials.

Case studies: Showcasing real-world examples of how your product or service has helped customers achieve their goals is another effective method. Case studies can be particularly compelling in industries where results can be measured, such as marketing or finance.

Influencer endorsements: Partnering with social media influencers who have a large following in your target audience is another way to leverage social proof. Influencers can promote your product or service to their followers, providing social proof through their endorsement.

Social media shares: Encouraging customers to share their experiences with your product or service on social media can help build credibility and trust with potential customers.

Awards and certifications: Displaying any awards or certifications that your product or service has received can help establish your brand as an authority in your industry, providing social proof to potential customers.

User-generated content: Sharing content created by your customers, such as photos or videos, can help build trust with potential customers by showcasing real people using and enjoying your product or service.

In conclusion, incorporating social proof into your sales strategy can help you establish trust and credibility with potential customers. Using customer testimonials, case studies, influencer endorsements, social media shares, awards and certifications, and user-generated content can provide social proof that your product or service is trustworthy and effective, ultimately helping you close deals quickly and build a loyal customer base.

Key #10: Build Trust With Testimonials

Testimonials can be a highly effective tool for establishing trust with potential customers. Essentially, they are statements from satisfied customers that speak to the quality and effectiveness of your product or service. You can showcase testimonials on your website, social media pages, or in marketing materials. Doing so can be an excellent way to demonstrate to potential customers that your brand is dependable and trustworthy.

When individuals read testimonials, they gain insight into the positive experiences that others have had with your product or service. This can be a crucial factor in building trust and credibility with potential customers, as they are more likely to put faith in the opinions of other customers over your brand's marketing messages. Additionally, testimonials can help to address any uncertainties or objections that potential customers may have about your product or service.

However, it is important to ensure that the testimonials you use are genuine and authentic. Avoid utilising phoney or paid testimonials, as they can be detrimental to your brand's reputation. Rather, request honest feedback from satisfied customers and use those testimonials to market your brand.

It is also important to select testimonials that are pertinent to your target audience. If you are targeting a particular niche or industry, it's wise to incorporate testimonials from customers in that field. Doing so can help to establish your brand as an authority in that industry and make it more appealing to potential customers.

Beyond traditional written testimonials, it may be worth considering video testimonials as well. Video testimonials can be more engaging and convincing than written ones, as they enable potential customers to see and hear directly from satisfied customers. Additionally, video testimonials can be shared on social media and other digital channels, increasing their reach and impact.

Overall, building trust with testimonials can be an effective way to quickly close deals and establish a loyal customer base. By using authentic and relevant testimonials, you can establish your brand as trustworthy and dependable while also addressing any uncertainties or objections that potential customers may have.

Chapter 3

Key #11: Use The Power Of Scarcity

Scarcity taps into people's fear of missing out (FOMO), making it a principle of psychology that can be used to create a sense of urgency in customers. This sense of urgency can motivate customers to act quickly to secure a rare or exclusive opportunity, which is particularly useful in sales.

One effective way to leverage scarcity in your sales process is by offering limited-time promotions or discounts. By setting a short window for the offer, such as a weekend sale, you create a sense of urgency that encourages customers to act quickly before the offer expires.

Limited quantity offers can also be effective. By offering a product or service that is only available to a specific number of customers, you can create a sense of exclusivity and urgency. This motivates customers to act quickly to secure the opportunity before it's gone.

Limited edition products are another way to use scarcity in your sales process. These products create a sense of rarity and exclusivity, which can make customers willing to pay more for a special or unique item.

Season or event-based offers can also be used to create urgency. By tying your offer to a specific event or season, such as offering discounts on gym memberships in January, you can motivate customers to take action quickly.

It's important to use scarcity ethically and transparently. Avoid creating false scarcity or using high-pressure sales tactics. Instead, focus on creating a genuine sense of urgency or exclusivity that adds value to your product or service. By doing so, you can use the power of scarcity to close deals quickly and ethically.

Key #12: Create A Sense Of Exclusivity

To market your product or service as exclusive, you can utilise a technique that creates a feeling of uniqueness and specialness among potential customers. This strategy sets your brand apart from competitors and can generate increased interest and desire to purchase.

One effective way to achieve a sense of exclusivity is by offering limited-time deals, such as time-sensitive discounts or special promotions available only to the first few buyers. This method generates a sense of urgency and scarcity, compelling customers to act quickly to take advantage of the offer.

Invite-only events are also an impactful approach to creating exclusivity. These exclusive gatherings are open only to a select group, imparting the feeling of being part of a unique and privileged community. These events can showcase products or services, provide valuable information or networking opportunities, or offer a distinctive experience.

Personalised offers tailored to the specific needs or interests of customers can also establish exclusivity. This approach can be particularly effective for luxury or high-end products or services, providing customers with the impression that they are receiving a unique and exclusive offering not available to everyone.

Membership programs that offer special benefits or rewards to members, such as exclusive access to events or products, can create a sense of exclusivity and belonging to a special group. This technique can foster brand loyalty and create a sense of community around your brand.

Overall, creating a sense of exclusivity can be a powerful way to differentiate your brand and drive customer interest and desire to buy. By making potential customers feel special and part of an exclusive group, you can build a devoted customer base and increase sales.

Key #13: Offer Guarantees

Providing guarantees is a reliable method of closing deals quickly since it addresses one of the primary concerns that customers have when making a purchase - the fear of making the wrong choice. Customers seek confidence that the product or service they are investing in will meet their needs and deliver the promised benefits. Offering a guarantee eliminates some of the risk from the purchasing process, granting customers peace of mind that they can test your product or service without worrying about losing their money.

Satisfaction guarantees are a popular type of guarantee as they assure customers that they can try the product or service without risk. This type of guarantee typically provides a complete refund if the customer is not satisfied with their purchase within a specific time frame. This guarantee encourages customers to make a purchase because they know they can test the product or service without the fear of losing their money if it fails to meet their expectations.

Performance guarantees are another effective type of guarantee because they assure customers that the product or service will perform as promised. This type of guarantee is particularly essential for products or services that require a significant investment of time, money, or effort. By providing a performance guarantee, you demonstrate confidence in your product or service and your willingness to stand by it.

Price guarantees are also effective as they assure customers that they are receiving the best possible value for their money. This guarantee motivates customers to make a purchase because they know they are getting a great deal. Price guarantees can also differentiate your product or service from competitors and provide a potent selling point.

Overall, offering guarantees is an effective approach to closing deals quickly as it addresses one of the primary concerns customers have when purchasing a product or service. By providing a guarantee, you alleviate some of the risk from the purchasing process, giving customers the confidence to try your product or service. This leads to faster sales, increased repeat business, and improved customer loyalty.

Key #14: Know When To Close The Deal

The ultimate goal of any sales pitch is to close the deal, but it requires a strategic and timely approach. Pushing too hard or too early can scare away the customer, while waiting too long can cause them to lose interest or seek a better deal elsewhere.

One clear indication that it's time to close the deal is when the customer has expressed interest in your product or service. This can be demonstrated by asking questions, offering comments, or showing a desire to learn more about what you offer. Such interest shows that they are open to making a purchase.

Another indicator that it's time to close the deal is when the customer has identified a need for your product or service. If they have shared a problem they're experiencing and you've shown them how your product can resolve the issue, it's a clear sign that they are ready to buy.

Pricing is also an essential factor that can suggest the customer is ready to make a purchase. If the customer is asking about pricing or comparing your prices to those of competitors, it's a sign that they are seriously considering making a purchase and want to ensure they are getting the best value for their money.

Positive body language is also a good sign that the customer is ready to buy. Nodding, smiling, and making eye contact show that they are engaged in the conversation and receptive to your pitch.

As the conversation is coming to a natural end, it's a good time to close the deal. However, it's important to be direct yet not pushy when asking for the sale. You can remind the customer of the benefits of your product or service and address any remaining concerns they may have.

Overall, recognizing the customer's signals and timing your pitch accordingly is crucial to closing the deal effectively and quickly.

Key #15: Don't Be Afraid To Ask For The Sale

The act of asking for the sale marks the culmination of all the preceding steps in the sales process. This is the point where you explicitly request the customer to take action and make a purchase. Although it may appear daunting, it is crucial to remember that asking for the sale is a customary component of the sales process and it is anticipated by the customer.

Asking for the sale demonstrates your belief in your product or service and your confidence that it can genuinely assist the customer. It also shows that you are committed to delivering a solution to their problem and that you stand behind your product or service.

A successful strategy for requesting a sale is to offer the customer a simple and straightforward selection between two options. For instance, after a conversation with the customer, you could suggest, "It seems like the deluxe package would best suit your needs. Would you like to move forward with that option, or do you have any additional questions?"

An additional approach is to ask for a commitment to proceed. An example of such a question is, "Would you be prepared to finalise this purchase today?" Asking this particular type of question has the ability to stimulate the customer to take prompt action and ultimately arrive at a decision.

It is crucial to be self-assured and straightforward while asking for the sale, while also being respectful of the customer's decision. If the customer is not yet prepared to make a decision, you can offer to provide additional information or address any remaining concerns. It is also essential to be transparent about the next steps and the purchase timeline.

To sum up, asking for the sale is a significant aspect of the sales process. By being confident, direct, and respectful, you can increase your likelihood of sealing the deal and establishing a long-term connection with the customer.

Chapter 4

Key #16: Make It Easy For The Customer To Say Yes

An important aspect of closing deals quickly is to make it easy for the customer to say yes. When the process is smooth and straightforward, customers are more likely to make a purchase and become satisfied with their experience.

There are several strategies to make it easy for customers to say yes:

Simplify the process: Provide clear instructions on how to make a purchase, minimise the number of steps involved, and remove any unnecessary obstacles that may cause hesitation or abandonment of the purchase.

Offer multiple payment options: By offering various payment methods like credit cards, PayPal, or other digital payment methods, customers can choose the option that suits them best, leading to an increased likelihood of purchase completion.

Provide clear instructions: By offering clear and concise instructions on how to complete the purchase, the process becomes more straightforward and less confusing. This may include step-by-step instructions or videos that walk the customer through the process.

Be available to answer questions: Being available to answer any customer questions can help build trust and confidence in the purchase. This may include providing additional information about the product or service, clarifying pricing or terms, or addressing any concerns the customer may have.

Follow up: After the sale, following up with the customer can ensure their satisfaction and address any concerns. This might include sending a thank-you note, providing additional resources or information, or offering support in the event of any issues or problems that may arise.

Overall, making it easy for customers to say yes is about creating a smooth, straightforward, and supportive experience that encourages them to make a purchase and become a satisfied customer. By being attentive, responsive, and proactive throughout the sales process, you can build a strong and loyal customer base and close deals quickly and efficiently.

Key #17: Follow Up Quickly And Consistently

Maintaining good relationships and closing deals depend on following up with your customers quickly and consistently. Prompt follow-up shows your commitment to meeting their needs and demonstrates that you value their time and input. Here are additional tips for effective follow-up:

Keep the conversation going: Quick follow-up after an initial meeting or conversation keeps the momentum going and demonstrates your commitment to their needs. This helps build trust and confidence in the relationship.

Show interest and engagement: Consistent follow-up shows your interest in the customer's needs and your commitment to finding the right solution for them. This helps build a positive relationship and establishes trust, a crucial factor in any sales process.

Offer additional information: Following up gives you an opportunity to provide additional information or address any questions the customer may have. This helps to alleviate concerns or doubts and increases confidence in the purchase decision.

Address concerns and objections: Following up also allows you to address any concerns or objections the customer may have. By responding thoughtfully and promptly, you can increase trust and confidence in the purchase decision and improve your chances of closing the deal.

Stay top-of-mind: Consistent follow-up helps keep you in the customer's thoughts, even if they are not yet ready to buy. This establishes a long-term relationship and opens up future opportunities for business.

In conclusion, following up quickly and consistently is crucial for successful sales. By staying engaged, responsive, and proactive throughout the sales process, you can build strong relationships, address concerns and objections, and close deals more efficiently.

Key #18: Celebrate Your Successes

Recognizing and celebrating your successes is crucial in all aspects of life, including quickly making sales. When you close a deal or make progress towards a sale, it's crucial to take a moment to acknowledge and celebrate your accomplishments. Doing so can help to build confidence and momentum, which can motivate you to continue working towards your objectives.

Here are some other reasons why celebrating your successes is essential:

Motivation: Celebrating your successes can help you stay motivated and energised. By building confidence and a sense of accomplishment, you can be propelled forward in your sales efforts.

Recognition: Celebrating your successes also provides an opportunity for recognition and validation from your peers, managers, and customers. This can help to build your reputation and establish you as a trustworthy and effective salesperson.

Reflection: Celebrating your successes can also help you reflect on what worked well and what didn't in your sales process. By identifying areas for improvement and refining your approach for future sales opportunities, you can enhance your performance and achieve better outcomes.

Team-building: Celebrating your successes as a team can help to build camaraderie and a sense of unity among your colleagues. This can foster a positive and collaborative work environment, which can lead to increased motivation and better sales outcomes.

Personal fulfilment: Finally, celebrating your successes is essential for your own personal fulfilment and well-being. Sales can be a challenging and high-pressure profession, and taking the time to acknowledge and celebrate your accomplishments can help to reduce stress and increase job satisfaction.

Overall, recognizing and celebrating your successes is a crucial part of the sales process. By staying motivated, reflective, and focused on your goals, you can build a successful and fulfilling career in sales.

Key #19: Continuously Improve Your Sales Process

To remain ahead of the competition and achieve long-term success, continuous improvement is essential for any salesperson. Here are several ways you can enhance your sales process continuously:

Analyse your performance: Regularly examine your sales performance to identify areas for improvement. Review your conversion rates, the length of your sales cycle, and your win/loss ratio to determine patterns and areas for improvement.

Solicit feedback: Request feedback from your customers on your sales process to discover what they liked and didn't like and where you can improve. This feedback can help you refine your approach and identify areas for improvement.

Stay informed: Stay current with the most recent industry trends, customer preferences, and sales techniques. Attend conferences, read industry publications, and network with other sales professionals to stay informed and learn new strategies.

Experiment: Try different sales techniques to determine which ones work best for you and your customers.

Test different approaches, scripts, and methods to see what resonates with your audience.

Embrace technology: Utilise tools like CRM software, sales automation software, and email marketing platforms to streamline your sales process and improve your results.

Invest in your skills: Continuously invest in your skills and knowledge as a sales professional. Attend training programs, read books, and take courses to remain up-to-date with the latest sales strategies and techniques.

Collaborate with others: Collaborate with other sales professionals to learn from each other and share best practices. Join industry associations, attend networking events, and participate in online forums to connect with other salespeople.

By continuously enhancing your sales process, you can stay ahead of the competition and achieve long-term success in your sales career.

Conclusion

Putting The Keys To Fast Sales Into Action

To apply the keys to fast sales, follow these steps:

Evaluate your current sales process: Scrutinise your sales process and pinpoint areas where you can implement the keys to fast sales. Determine which keys are most applicable to your business and customers.

Develop a sales plan: Create a sales plan that integrates the keys to fast sales. Define your sales objectives, target audience, and sales strategy, and outline your sales process from start to finish.

Train your sales team: Ensure that your sales team understands the keys to fast sales and how to use them. Offer training and coaching to enhance their sales skills and techniques.

Implement the keys to fast sales: Apply the keys to fast sales in your sales process. Use tactics like creating scarcity, establishing rapport with customers, asking the right questions, and highlighting your unique selling points.

Evaluate your results: Assess your sales outcomes frequently to determine the effectiveness of your sales process. Analyse your conversion rates, sales cycle length, and other metrics to identify areas where you can make improvements.

Continuously enhance your sales process: Continually refine your sales process by seeking feedback, testing new strategies, and investing in your sales skills and knowledge.

By putting the keys to fast sales into practice, you can boost your sales results and achieve your sales objectives. Although it requires time and effort, the benefits are well worth it.